CLEANING UP IN A DIRTY BUSINESS

Make Money Fast by Starting a Janitorial Company

CORA SCHUPP

Copyright © 2014 by Cora Schupp
15 16 17 18 19   5 4 3 2 1
All rights reserved. No part of this book may be reproduced, stored in a retrieval system or transmitted, in any form or by any means, without the prior written consent of the publisher or a licence from The Canadian Copyright Licensing Agency (Access Copyright). For a copyright licence, visit www.accesscopyright.ca or call toll free 1-800-893-5777.

Curve Communications
www.curvecommunications.com
Cartoons copyright © Mark Parisi and TheJanitorialStore.com. Reprinted with permission.

Library and Archives Canada Cataloguing in Publication
Schupp, Cora, 1957–, author Cleaning up in a dirty business: make money fast by starting a janitorial company / Cora Schupp.

Issued in print and electronic formats.
ISBN 978-0-9684322-2-8 (pbk.) – ISBN 978-0-9684322-3-5 (html)
1. Building cleaning industry–Management. 2. House cleaning–Management. 3. New business enterprises. I. Title.
HD9999.B882S38 2015 648'.5068 C2014-907116-7 C2014-907117-5
ISBN 978-0-9684322-2-8 (paperback)
ISBN 978-0-9684322-3-5 (ebook)

I am dedicating this book to Hans Schupp, without whose unflinching loyalty to me this past decade, I would not have been able to walk on many a stormy sea.

I also dedicate this book to my three beautiful children, Sasha, Chelsea, and Alexander.

I did the very best I knew how.

CONTENTS

	Acknowledgements	vii
1.	Why Owning a Janitorial Company Is a Great Idea!	1
2.	Getting Started	6
3.	Legalities	12
4.	Cleaning Duties	19
5.	Staffing/Human Resources	23
6.	Marketing	36
7.	Accounting	44
8.	Quoting	50
9.	Managing	54
10.	Trouble Shooting And Problem Solving	61
11.	Keeping Personal Relationships Intact	63
12.	Challenges	65

13.	My Own Story Of Struggles And Success	69
14.	Action Plan	78
	Templates	83
	Resources	85
	Conclusion	91

ACKNOWLEDGEMENTS

I wish to acknowledge George Affleck and Amanda Bates, owners of Curve Communications Group Ltd. for their unwavering support of the writing of this book. I also wish to thank Kerry Slater and Justin Wong for their copy editing and technical guidance, and Trena White of Page Two Strategies for her encouragement and patience through the many writes and rewrites. The whole project has been great fun.

CHAPTER 1.

WHY OWNING A JANITORIAL COMPANY IS A GREAT IDEA!

After years of running a janitorial service company, I found myself among the top 5% of female wage earners in Canada, earning $90,000 per year in 2004 (and my husband pulling an equal share) with no post-secondary education. I had contracts with a chain of department stores and 13 grocery superstores. I had over 100 employees working for me and was my own boss. I built my company from scratch – and so can you.

How did I get my start? Newly married in a small northern town named Kitimat, BC, in the late 1970s, my husband and I scraped together a down payment on a house by doing janitorial work in the evening. The contractor who built our house also had a janitorial service, so we both worked full-time during the day and rushed to our evening jobs after a quick dinner. We dreamt of moving to the Lower Mainland of British Columbia, where there were better educational opportunities for our children, more social and cultural advantages, and better weather.

After a couple of years, we decided that the only way we could leave Kitimat was to gain some experience owning a small company. We started cleaning apartments that had been vacated, then we moved on to construction cleanup, before finally picking up a couple of small contracts. I was nine months pregnant when I dropped off our first signed contract! It was for cleaning the offices of a natural gas company. I did all the bookkeeping for our small business, which included payroll, taxes, Workers' Compensation, etc. Eventually we sold our company for a healthy profit and took the plunge to the Lower Mainland.

We moved to Surrey, BC, in 1986, right before the World Exposition, or EXPO, started. We bought a small existing janitorial company that included an old truck, a buffing machine, some odds and sods of mops and buckets, and two little contracts. Buying this company turned out to be a good investment because we did such a great job that the clients were happy to be our references. Within three months we were grossing $10,000 a month.

From these small beginnings, we took on contracts with the chain stores. We were able to save for our retirement, educate our children, own a lovely home with property, and we still had time to travel.

I decided to write this book in an effort to help those of you who have always dreamed of owning your own business but didn't know where to start. If you use my model for success, you will be well on your way to becoming a business owner. The type of person who had "to do everything the hard way," I can save you not only money but also a lot of stress and heartache by sharing my own experiences.

Why a janitorial service? It is one of the few businesses that neither depends on a thriving economy nor suffers the ups and downs of a seasonal or fickle market. It does not require a lot of startup capital or a lot of training. Although janitorial duties are not glamorous, all businesses need to keep clean. Believe me, you will never run out of work.

The ability to set your own hours and work schedule is invaluable. Running a janitorial company doesn't tie you down to a monotonous Monday to Friday, 9 am – 5 pm routine. As long as the job is done, most clients don't care what time you come (unless they are locked at certain times). It is never boring because each place is different, and each client has different needs.

You can schedule your clients around your own personal life instead of the other way around. Once your team is trained, you can move forward and take on more clients, which frees you up later in life to do the quoting, ordering, hiring and training, and leave the heavier work for younger folk. That way you can be in control of your retirement.

There is dignity in service, and you are not just the "cleaning lady" or the "janitor" but a self-employed tax-paying business owner, creating jobs and contributing to society.

You may be questioning whether you have what it takes to run a successful company, so let's look at a few urban legends out there.

"You need an education." You do need to be able to read, write and do math. Computer skills like using spreadsheets and word processing are necessary but can be obtained through short courses at local colleges. Most of your education will be the school of hard knocks, with a degree of Trial and Error 101 thrown in.

"**Thousands out there are looking for work.**" You aren't thousands; you are only one, but a special and unique individual that no one can replace.

"**4 out of 5 businesses fail.**" Yes that is true, but that also means 1 out of 5 does succeed and yours is going to be that one!

"**You are too old/young.**" Don't even get me started on this one.

"**You need connections.**" What you *actually* need is to start out small, get a good reputation, and build on it. Success doesn't come overnight, but everyone has the right to make a living and prospective customers respect that. Once your business is growing, connections will come naturally.

A good work ethic is more important than money or education. Constancy is a virtue that is very important in your path to success; those who are grounded, secure, and committed to long-term goals will reach their ultimate vision.

That vision or destination might be a secure retirement, a good lifestyle, enough money for your children's education, or just self-satisfaction. The goal is different for everyone, but the end results are the same: a well-run, sustainable business that can later be sold or handed down to the next generation.

MY PROMISE TO YOU

My promise is that if you take the information in this

book to heart, you will be well on your way to being a successful businessperson. You already have everything you need to succeed; you just need to fulfill your own potential. The fact that you invested in my book already shows that you are willing to take action.

CHAPTER 2.

GETTING STARTED

Before launching your business, you should ask yourself a few pointed questions: Are you in a good position financially and physically at this time in your life? Do you want to focus on offices, stores, or homes? Are you willing and able to do some of the dirty work yourself in the beginning or when problems suddenly come up? Are you able to work evenings and weekends? Once you have a sense of what appeals to you most, you will get a sense of direction.

So, what next? Every business (not just a janitorial one) is a baby that never grows up. It constantly needs to be fed, nurtured, and tended. The sooner you think of that business as a separate entity, the better. It is now a separate person in the room with its own quirks and personality. Keep your baby nourished by doing your research, keeping the business simple, and growing naturally. A baby can't run before it can walk, and neither should your business. You *will* make mistakes, but believe me, you will get right back up again. Every mistake you make in the beginning will give you valuable knowledge and experience.

If you keep in mind that there is a tremendous learning curve in the beginning, it will be easier to avoid becoming discouraged. The results will definitely be worth the effort.

Let's begin with the basics of starting your business.

MISSION STATEMENT

This is a waste of time. I worked for a company who worked for months on their mission statement. It gets tacked to the wall and no one looks at it again. You are on your own mission and make your own statement.

CREATE A BUSINESS PLAN

You can download a template from the internet and fill it in yourself. I suggest one named "Plan Genie." (Please refer to my Resources chapter for a link.) This will guide you through the process of how to run your day-to-day business, your goals, your prospective market, and the types of financial reports you will generate. We didn't have a business plan ourselves when we started our company; we just did whatever came under our nose for the day. Looking back, I wish that I had taken some time to develop a clearer idea of what I wanted. Maybe I wouldn't have felt so often that I was fumbling around in the dark looking for the light switch.

You will also impress your new best friend (the bank manager!) if you have a business plan. Even if life doesn't go according to plan at the end of the year, it does show that you put some thought into it. More importantly, you will show the bank manager that you didn't wake up one morning and just decide you were going to be rich and famous by running a dirty business.

CREATE A BUDGET

Just like a home budget, this is a great tool to watch your profit and loss. It will change from day to day and month to month as you grow, but it does give a baseline to work from. Factor in labor, equipment maintenance, etc. and look at it every month so see where you need to make adjustments. It may look completely different at the end of the year, but by the second year you will have a better handle on your numbers and be able to predict your costs and income more accurately. You will see very quickly that if you eliminate an office and its associated expenses, it leaves a lot more profit. You have to generate around $25,000 – $30,000 per month before you should even consider an outside office. Do as much as you can, as long as you can, around your home and garage with a PO box. The same applies to hiring staff, so play around with the numbers on this budget to get a feel of the realities of profit and loss. A sample budget is on the microsite coraschupp.com

MAKE A LIST OF LEADS

I give further information on this in Chapter 6: Marketing, but put some ideas on paper and start a database of contacts.

START-UP CASH

This is part of budgeting, but do your research and planning to see what your costs will be. Go window shopping at a few janitorial or vacuum supply stores, look online, etc. Unlike most other businesses that require a storefront or expensive equipment, a janitorial service needs only a little cash investment. You will be putting your time, energy and labor into it initially, and can slowly build up your equipment and supplies as you go. You won't need thousands of dollars in the beginning, that's for sure.

STAFFING

Take an honest look at your current lifestyle as this changes the dynamics of your company. Do you want to hire staff right away? My next question, then, is "What is your tolerance for pain?" All kidding aside, gain confidence in doing the job yourself, with maybe just a helper, and then start to hire a full team.

SPECIALIZING

Do you already have certain skill sets, such as carpet or window cleaning? If so, that is great but don't let a lack of skills hold you back as you can start out with general cleaning at first.

NAMING YOUR COMPANY

You will want to come up with a name that is catchy and will not be outdated in a few years. Our first company was named "Spic and Span Janitorial." Our next one was "Masterpiece Floor Maintenance Ltd." and I came up with a logo of an artist's palette and brush. The logo was easy to design and reflected our attitude towards making sure the end result was a sparkling, waxed, and polished floor. The brush was a stylized mop, since of course after the floor was polished, it looked like a masterpiece!

Look into choosing company colors to go on your van and stationary, but don't go all out on expenses right away. If you don't have the resources or ability to get a logo designed, do it yourself and get the printers to clean it up for you. Many will offer that service for a small fee to get your business. As an alternative, why not approach a local college and see if an undergraduate will take on the job?

OFFICE SPACE

Don't get an office space right away; remember, you want to start slow. A PO box number is fine but never use your home address or give out your home number. Most janitorial work takes place in the evenings and weekends and you should respect the privacy of your home and family. This is more relevant now than 20 years ago, with heightened interest in security and escalating crime. Your home is sacred – don't ever forget it.

Secure a phone number that is easy for you and your clients to remember, i.e. 555-SPOT. Don't create a website right away unless that is your hidden talent. Those things all come later.

Now that you have thought all of this through, LET'S GET STARTED!

CLEANING UP IN A DIRTY BUSINESS 11

CHAPTER 3.

LEGALITIES

The old saying goes, "The job isn't finished until the paperwork is done," and unfortunately this is still true today. Don't let the paperwork intimidate you, as it is all common sense and you just need to work through each item one by one. I have listed everything in chronological order so nothing gets missed.

REGISTERING YOUR COMPANY

Once you have chosen your business name, register it with your state or province. You can usually register a company name online. Don't make the mistake of working hard for years to build up your brand only to have your competitors snatch it right out from under your nose and register it themselves. It's helpful to have two other backup names ready in case yours is already taken.

What is the difference between registering and incorporating? When you first start out, you need to legally register your business with your local province or state. You can run it as a sole proprietor, which means you're self-employed. Once you get larger, you may want to incorporate the company, which makes it a legal entity and separates your personal worth from your business or corporate worth. That is useful if you have personal assets like your house that are tied to the company, or if you loaned personal money to the company, because it gives you some protection in case anything goes wrong. It can cost around a thousand dollars to incorporate, so save yourself that expense until you become profitable.

Obtain a business license at your local city hall. It will feel good to become a person of substance and it is essential from a legal point of view.

TAXES

If you're in Canada, apply for a GST (Goods and Service Tax) number right away. It is also your business number, which you will need in order to pay your taxes and legally operate your janitorial service. In the U.S., you need to apply for a Federal Tax ID. Please refer to the Resources chapter for links.

You don't have to charge GST until you make your first $30,000 (as of 2014), but it looks more professional if you do. GST is not an expense to you; you only collect the money and subtract any GST you may have paid on any business-related purchases. This only applies for Canada but those English-speaking people from other countries have similar taxes, but under different names.

You won't need a PST (Provincial Sales Tax) number because you are not re-selling products. Unfortunately that means any PST paid will be absorbed as an expense (i.e. wax, stripper, soap, mops) so remember to build that into your quotations. As of 2014, it is 7% in BC and each province does charge it, although at different rates. This is a big chunk of coin to lose if you don't account for it; it will definitely show up on your bottom line.

Here's how to pick out a tax rate for any given quote. Let's say the quote is $158.00 and the tax rate is 7%. I have found the following simple formula very useful and use it daily even today, self-employed doing accounting and business consulting. The same principle holds for any rate:

1. Multiply your quote by 7.
2. Divide by 107.
3. This equals $10.34.
4. Subtract this number from your original quote and you will have your subtotal of $147.66.

Now you know what your hard cost is, if you are quoted a price with "tax included." This is also very important when you get your credit card statement at the end of the month and some of your receipts are missing. You want to get the input tax credit for your GST return, and this way you can segregate the hard cost with the tax. Input Tax Credit, or ITC, is the GST *paid on purchases* as opposed to GST *collected on sales*. You may wish to keep them in separate ledgers in your accounting, to make it clear how much you collected and how much you paid out. You subtract what you paid from what you collected, and submit the difference to Canada Revenue Agency (CRA).

You can deduct business expenses like rent, utilities, insurance, payroll, etc. when you file your income taxes, which helps reduce the taxes you pay to the government. But don't get too carried away with tax-deductible receipts. The expense that most people abuse is entertainment.

Buying yourself a $5.00 coffee from Starbucks because

you weren't organized enough to make it at home is not a tax deduction. Neither is going through the drive-thru at McDonalds because you were too mentally lazy or busy to pack a meal or you had to take the kids to hockey practice. Canada Revenue Agency and the United States Internal Revenue Service are of the opinion that you have to eat whether you are in business or not. Sorry, but taking yourself out for coffee to discuss business in your head does not count as a tax write-off.

If you take a client out for coffee or a meal, on the other hand, the receipt will be for two or more people and that's not a problem as long as you mark the receipt as such for your files.

WORKERS' COMPENSATION

In Canada, most employers are required to have a Workers' Compensation Board (WCB) number. Your WCB number is very important. It is called WorkSafe in BC and it is the law. The U.S. equivalent is called Workers' Compensation.

Once you apply for your account, you will be informed of your premium. You may be billed yearly at first, based on the percentage of the previous year's salary. There is a maximum cap but it's quite high so it is doubtful any of your employees will make that. The premium will go down every year that you don't have a major accident or claim.

Workers' Compensation is needed in case any of your employees gets injured on the job; their wages will be at least partially covered while they heal.

You can choose to opt out of paying yourself as a business owner but it doesn't hurt to pay a minimum amount in case you get hurt on the job yourself. As a self-employed person, you probably won't have any medical coverage or unemployment benefits. You need to pay your WCB fees diligently because most reputable potential clients will request a letter of clearance from WCB for your company.

Adhere to safety standards and your WCB premium will lessen every year. Book some time each month with your employees (and pay them for their time) to review basics like lifting heavy objects properly, mixing chemicals, using goggles and gloves, wiping up wet spots, picking up cords and cables, using a ladder properly, and following other safety guidelines. Just one second of not being "aware of your surroundings" can permanently injure an employee. Believe me, you don't want that on your conscience.

WCB is not the enemy. They are an invaluable resource for both safety and health and also offer free resources like posters and a newsletter. See the Resources chapter for a link to register for WCB.

Again, for those out-of-country readers, these links will familiarize you with the processes and you should have no problem finding the appropriate one for your country.

INSURANCE

Larger companies will want their janitorial providers to have at least $5,000,000 in liability insurance in case someone slips and falls on your lovely clean floor. And believe me, someone will. Some people make a living out of scamming insurance companies on dubious incidents, and most insurance companies would rather pay up than fight a long and costly claim.

These companies will also want your employees bonded. That doesn't mean individually, but a blanket premium that must be paid in case an employee steals on the job, etc.

Dictionary.com defines bonding as "an insurance contract in which an agency guarantees payment to an employer in the event of unforeseen financial loss through the actions of an employee." Unfortunately, it does happen in every industry.

How important is bonding? "The latest statistics we have show that one-third of all bankruptcies are caused by employee theft," says Marc Leclair, former Assistant Vice President of Corporate Risk with London Guarantee in Toronto, Ontario.

Shop around and get quotes on liability insurance. Find an insurance agent who can clearly explain the technicalities and has experience insuring your line of business.

It is very common for a customer to request both a WCB letter of clearance and proof of liability insurance before any contract is signed. It looks good when you submit them promptly, so you should have these documents in place before they're needed.

CONTRACTS

A good contract template can also be downloaded, but remember to keep it simple for both parties. A blank contract is not worth the paper it is written on, but two inked signatures and a date make it legally binding. Always keep a signed copy on file under lock and key so no one can discover your company "secrets" and use this information to poach contracts from you.

A statement of work, outlining the scope of the job you will be doing, can either be attached or added separately. Make sure the statements are specific, for example, dusting daily, garbage weekly, windows monthly, etc. It serves as protection on both sides to have expectations in writing.

Hiring a lawyer if a client does renege on a contract is time consuming and costly, and as the old saying goes, "You can't get blood from a turnip." If an issue arises, it is better to just drop it and carry on with the next potential client. I know a lot of people feel hurt and angry, and want a sense of justice, so they will hire a lawyer "on principle" but take it from me, swallow your pride because the lawyers will be dancing on your grave after the money is spent. That may seem harsh but it is sound advice.

To see and download a simple contract, please visit my website, http://coraschupp.com. It is simple, clear, and understandable and has a thirty-day termination clause, which may or may not be useful to you.

CHAPTER 4.

CLEANING DUTIES

Floors need to be swept and mopped, and once you are in the big leagues, they will need to be scrubbed and polished as well. It is easiest to break the layout of the floor into sections. Depending how busy the traffic is at the store, each section needs to be stripped of old wax, re-waxed, and polished. Obviously high-frequency areas will need to be done more often as the wax will wear off. Rotate a different section weekly so the whole floor is redone over six months. Each section needs to be done when no one will track over it – so obviously it has to be done at night when no one else is around.

Some of our clients requested to lock the staff in at night. I didn't like that at all and would only agree if there was a safety exit in case of fire or emergency. I also wouldn't agree if the end of shift was so late that there was no transit and our female employees would have to walk home in the dark.

If the client doesn't care about your employees' safety, then fire them. I know that sounds funny, but I have fired clients who were abusive to my staff or wanted them to work in unsafe conditions. You are not hungry enough to need clients like that, believe me. Someone else will come along who values your work ethic and commitment to your employees. My colleagues have heard me say many times, "Your employees are your greatest assets."

Our business specialized in floor maintenance. When we first started, most of the floors were vinyl, but nowadays they can be terrazzo, ceramic, concrete, or wood. Make sure you go to your supplier and get the best cleaning products and training for each floor type before you arbitrarily start slopping chemical on your customer's floor. Please make sure that there is always some friction in the wax you are applying so the floors aren't too slippery. The label should indicate that, but ask your supplier for the right one to match your customer's floor so you get the right balance of friction and shine.

Before the doors open and people come in, take a last look to make sure there are no puddles, produce, or other items left on the floor. They are just accidents waiting to happen and accidents will be one of your largest worries. You definitely don't want your lack of care to cause an injury.

To download a sample cleaning schedule/checklist, please visit my website.

CLEANING SUPPLIES

Some basic cleaning supplies can be purchased at stores like Costco or Walmart, but make sure you get your vacuum cleaners, scrubbers, buffers, carpet cleaners, etc. from a cleaning supplier who can fix it *when* (not if) it breaks down. As my mom always said, "Buy the best you can afford." The supplier will also give you suggestions on cleaners and different solutions to stubborn cleaning problems.

Find yourself a supplier that is close by so you don't have to waste time and gas driving around to pick up your supplies. Also make sure they are knowledgeable and interested in you.

I wish that we lived in a perfect world, where ecologically-friendly cleaning supplies really existed. The ones on the market right now just don't work as well as standard cleaning supplies and are much more expensive. Of course, a lot can be done with vinegar and baking soda. Vinegar is still the best for cleaning windows since it doesn't leave streaks. So is non-sudsy ammonia. The Dutch have a saying that "the best cleanser is water," and you don't argue with the Dutch about cleanliness; they have it in the bag.

We also said in the industry that cleaning involves four things. If you take one item away, it won't work.

1. Water
2. Cleanser
3. Heat
4. Friction

In other words, good old-fashioned hot soapy water and elbow grease.

CHAPTER 5.

STAFFING/HUMAN RESOURCES

In the beginning you will do most of the work yourself, or if you are lucky, get family members to work with you. However, you may have to hire staff soon, which entails a lot more responsibility. This might be a few weeks, or a few months. You won't make any real money unless you grow to the point that you hire staff, because you can only work 24 hours a day. After that you are making your profit on their man-hours.

Of course, if you don't want the stress and hassle of employees, by all means keep your company small. You may require that situation for this time in your life.

It's important to know the job yourself inside and out, since you can't expect your employees to follow suit. If a client complained and I looked at a job, I had to ask myself honestly, "Could I have done it better myself?" If the answer was yes, the employee needed more training. I suggest training your crew to do each job, leaving a reliable staff member behind to lead the crew, and then taking one of the key players forward to the next contract until he/she is ready to lead his/her own team. Don't spread yourself too thin.

PAYROLL: A WORKER IS WORTHY OF HIS WAGES

Once you hire staff, you will have to do payroll, which entails withholding their pension, employment insurance and taxes, and remitting them to the government in a timely manner. I recommend paying twice a month (as opposed to every two weeks), with a mid-month advance (approximately half of their income after taxes, a round figure). That way you only have to figure out the tax deductions once a month, which saves you some hassle. Paying employees twice a month, rather than every two weeks, is also easier on job costing, as it follows the calendar better. If you pay every two weeks, you are always accruing wages to get them in line monthly, which is more complicated than you want it to be. You will probably be billing monthly, so your costs will follow monthly.

If you can afford it, eventually you might be able to pay for a medical/dental plan for your employees. You can either pay all the premiums, or the employee can pay half. We tried to get a retirement plan going, but it had to be an all or nothing plan and the employees didn't want it. It was a shame and shortsighted on their part but at least we offered.

You will also have to pay out vacation pay; in Canada employers have to give a minimum of 2 weeks, or 4% of an employee's gross salary. That amount has to be paid out either when the employee leaves the company or when they go on holidays. Keep a spreadsheet to track your employees' time off. Include sick days and banked days on that form. Refer to the Resources chapter for information on vacation pay requirements.

SEARCHING FOR EMPLOYEES

When you're ready to search for employees, you can use your local job bank associated with the employment insurance office; it's free. The Resources chapter has links for job banks in both Canada and the United States.

Don't waste money on newspaper ads as they are costly and take too long to print. Craigslist is okay but I am not a fan of that site as it looks unprofessional and there are a lot of scammy postings. Sorry, Craig.

All prospective employers are fishing out of the same sea: the one you see when you look out the window. The same people looking for work will look at both the paid sites and the free ones, so save some money and time. In addition to the job banks, try your local Chamber of Commerce website, as they usually have free links to employment sites. Don't pay headhunter fees; they are very expensive and they do the same job that you would on your own for a minimal investment of time.

You will get a lot of resumes, but scan them carefully for suitability. Do they have experience? Is the resume written with proper spelling and punctuation? You may think I am an elitist, but in this day and age everyone has spell-check. A poorly-written resume is a sign of laziness that will undoubtedly reflect on job performance. Even if English is a person's second language, the resume can still be tidy.

You can download a simple application form on my website, http://coraschupp.com, and modify it with your own company name and logo. There were times when we were so desperate for workers I only got a napkin with a name, phone number, birth date and social insurance number scribbled on it, but that was enough to get them on payroll. The prospective employee will probably come with a resume for their interview, but the application form is needed after your decide to hire that person, as they will need to give their social insurance number so you can withhold payroll deductions, and most people don't put that type of information freely on the resume.

I have worked in offices since then that almost require you to own a wheelbarrow to carry all the paperwork your employees need to fill in after they are hired. I always thought that was ridiculous. Many employees come from other countries where English is a second language, and while I know there are a lot of legal responsibilities, these forms should be more reasonable.

You can't ask for age or gender anymore on an application form, but I will share a funny story with you. One gentleman was stymied over the question SEX:_____ or _____, which meant you had to fill in either male or female.

His response? "Yes, once in Kamloops."

My last story on this subject is about the wonderful middle-aged gentleman who, once he completed the application form, proudly pulled out a certificate from BC Mental Health, stating that he was no longer mentally ill!

CHECKING REFERENCES

Some prospective employees will exaggerate their claims, so it is always useful to check references. References must be supervisors in companies they have worked for, not friends, relatives or landlords. Always demand three work references, and their landlord doesn't count! I can't stress enough the importance of doing due diligence and getting proper referrals.

When you phone a reference, don't be surprised if the person in Human Resources seems hesitant to give answers. These days everyone is afraid of getting sued for slander. Sometimes what is not said is louder than what is said, so try to chat with the person on the other line for awhile. Ask if they have time to talk, and identify yourself and your company. If they are also business owners, they won't want to recommend a bad employee either.

These are some of the questions you might ask a reference:

1. What responsibilities did the candidate have while working at your company?
2. Do you think the candidate is qualified to assume the responsibilities of the position you are filling? Why or why not?
3. How would you describe your management style? (This seems like a strange question, but think about it, your prospective employee might respond to a different style and this question will give you some insight into the candidate's personality.)
4. How did the candidate perform with regard to performance/punctuality/ability to follow directions/ability to problem solve?
5. Is this person a team player, or does he/she excel working alone?
6. What was the candidate's attendance record? Was the candidate on time and dependable?
7. What challenges or opportunities for growth were offered to the candidate and how did he or she respond?
8. What are the candidate's three strongest qualities?

9. What was the candidate's reason for leaving the position?
10. Would you rehire this candidate?

I was once recruiting for a mechanic in a previous job and received a fabulous resume from someone in Toronto who wanted to move to Vancouver. There were diplomas attached and the references were all glowing, but I had a suspicious feeling about them. I printed the references out and laid them side-by-side on my desk. Only then did I notice the font and writing styles were all the same. When I looked up the companies, I discovered that the addresses were non-existent or the person referring had already been retired for years. It was obvious the applicant had downloaded the logos and written the references himself. When I confronted him, he became verbally abusive and threatening.

Can you image if I had hired him and he got upset with me? He could literally throw a monkey wrench in our operation and destroy all our equipment. My boss was thrilled with me. He said in 36 years in business he had never been hoodwinked like that.

I have a very sad story to relate: four days after I gave birth to my son, one of the managers of a grocery store that we cleaned phoned to tell us that a bunch of lottery tickets had been stolen and that all evidence pointed to our only employee on site at the time. They phoned the police and we arranged to go to the employee's home a little before the police arrived.

My husband said: "Buddy, the police are coming. Quickly, show me where you hid the stolen tickets."

The employee took him to the garage and moved a ceiling tile and pulled out the tickets. The police came and arrested him on the spot with the evidence in his hand. You might think that this was a dirty trick but we had to think of our own contract, reputation, and livelihood. The store manager's wife and I sat in the car and watched while the employee was handcuffed and taken away. His wife and kids were bawling. I started crying too and had to be comforted by the store manager's wife, who was also crying. It was all too much.

Let me remind you again, as this was the hard lesson we learned: CHECK AT LEAST THREE REFERENCES. There was an old radio station that related human interest stories, and the tag line was, "Who knows what goes on in the hearts of men? The Shadow Knows." Unfortunately, you will never really know what goes on in the hearts of people and there is no real way to factor out dishonesty.

HIRING DECISIONS

Once you do hire someone, you have three months to see whether they'll work out; after that it becomes extremely difficult to let someone go. Not just emotionally (no one likes to fire someone), but you have to pay severance pay, usually two weeks plus another week for every year worked. If not, you'll have to deal with an unjust dismissal claim against you that will cost you lots of money and grief.

We once had two people on staff who met on a job site, fell in love and got married. They have raised children together and are still very happily married. However, we did not like to hire couples or members of the same family. It isn't that we don't believe in family, but if there is a wedding or funeral in their home, they will both need time off. If they get into a car accident and they are together, they are both hurt. If the flu goes around, they are both sick. The end result is that you're scrambling to fill two spots, which isn't fair to the rest of the staff.

After a few years, we found it helped to include one of our supervisors in the hiring decision. Letting your supervisors have this authority is beneficial because they know their crew better than anyone and they are the ones who will have to work with the employee eight hours a day. If he recommended friends or relatives, I would consider them as well. A crew that gets along and works well together is invaluable.

You may be able to access grants or government subsidies for your staff through the local employment agencies that handle employment insurance claims. Most will reimburse you a portion of the minimum wage after submitting claim forms and proof of payment. As always, be careful whom you hire. Your company can go downhill quickly if you hire people who don't show up, show up drunk, or steal from the client.

I once had a successful applicant who came from Romania. He swam across the Danube at night under threat of gunfire (many years ago under a different regime), and I figured if he had that much gumption, he would work hard for us. He proved me right.

Another young lady whom I ended up hiring was asked to fill out the necessary forms from the government so I could get an employment subsidy. When she came to the question, "Are you a visible minority?" she asked, "Cora, what does this mean? There is nothing wrong with my eyesight." Sigh...

MY SECRETS TO SUCCESS IN MAINTAINING HUMAN RESOURCES

These are the biggest lessons I have learned and I am now sharing them with you.

Your Employees Are Your Best Assets

Never forget that your most valuable asset is not your contracts, your equipment, or your vehicle. It is your staff. Always, *always* treat them with respect, dignity, and pay them higher than the market rate. It is a lot cheaper in the long run to pay someone a little bit more; they are more likely to stay with you and you won't have to continually train and churn out new staff, who will make mistakes. Besides, low pay can lead to low morale. I heard a quote the other day that made me laugh: "If you only pay peanuts, you will get monkeys working for you."

Always compliment your employees on a job well done and treat them once in a while to coffee or lunch.

The reality is that you make your living off of their backs; this is capitalism 101. Yes, you take risks by running a company, but they have to scrub the yucky toilets and dirty floors.

A company that keeps its staff for years speaks well for itself. I am still in touch with my administrative assistant, ten years after working with her. She eventually bought another company I owned. We worked together side by side and watched our children grow up together, and we were there for each other when our parents died. There is no dollar value to this type of relationship, as no one knows you better than someone who spends eight hours a day with you for years and years.

Paper Trail, Paper Trail, Paper Trail!

Memories are short and notoriously unreliable. Someone is continually late? Diarize their late appearances in a calendar. You had to give someone a verbal warning? Write it down. Yes, those contradict the phrase "verbal warning," but always keep a couple of short paragraphs in the employee's file. I liked to record the date, transgression, witnesses, etc. This will be invaluable later if you need to let someone go. There will always be a lot of "he said, she said" but if there is a paper trail, there is no doubt. Keep these files under lock and key.

If you do have to give someone a verbal warning, do everyone a favor and take that person into your office and tell him or her quietly and privately. Leave the door slightly ajar so no one can start yelling or accuse you of being inappropriate.

I have a recipe for giving criticism that I call the "mayonnaise sandwich." Let's use the example of someone who is chronically late, which holds up the client and can mean the rest of the staff has to work overtime.

First step: a slice of bread: non-threatening, bland.

"How are you, how are the kids, how's the weather, etc."

Then, add a generous amount of jam to make your feedback sweet and easy to swallow.

You have been with us how long? That is great; you are a valuable member of the team. I remember when you... Or when you helped with ...

Now a very thin layer of mayonnaise (sour, not so nice with the jam).

We have been having some reports of you being late. I know you have been having trouble with ... or that ... but it has come to the point that I have to bring it up. What can we do together that can solve that problem right away?

Finally, the last layer of soft, bland bread.

"How about those Canucks?"

You get the drift. You can change the recipe to meet your needs but the whole thing should still be easy to digest. Your staff member isn't stupid; they will get the point while still retaining their dignity.

Overtime

This was and always will be a sticky question. As an employer you have to pay overtime, but if your client wants coverage on a 10-hour shift with only five people per shift, you will quickly go broke. Overtime means anything over 8 hours per day, or more than 40 hours per week. To make it work, I relied on a rotating shift with the employees where they worked three 12-hour shifts and three off. That way they worked 36 hours a week. Once the staff had approved it, I took the schedule to the Ministry of Labor and got a Variance Permit. See the Resources chapter for links.

This permit is not easy to get as the Ministry protects employees from potential abuse (and rightly so). Because I came forward with the schedule and had it signed off, I was given the permit without too much of a hassle. If you are in a similar situation, please do this, as janitorial duties are usually performed after hours.

I worked out the employee schedules a month at a time and handed them out well in advance so the employees knew their shifts. I also included all pertinent phone numbers of employees and clients' managers or supervisors, and kept plenty of copies flying around in the van, home, and office. Of course, those were the days before smart phones. Always keep your information up to date so you don't have to scramble for phone numbers if you're called at 3 am because someone didn't show up, supplies ran out, or a vehicle or equipment broke down.

People asked me over the years about how to meet the challenges of staffing and "no-shows."

If you have to fire someone just before a shift – what do you do then? Try your best to cross-train your team ahead of time, and have someone available on call, or a float, which is a temporary worker who can be kept busy with holiday/maternity/sick relief. If you have a small crew, you may have to jump in yourself, or with a larger crew, they will be one man short. Reward them in some way to thank them for being short staffed (after all, you did save a night's pay) and make your team feel it was worth pulling together.

Sometimes, employees would want to exercise their right to party. This resulted in them coming in to work hungover, late, or not at all. The rest of the crew had to work harder to make up for it. To deal with frequent offenders, we had a "three strikes and you're out" policy.

Subcontractors

A lot of janitorial services like to use subcontractors. You have to be careful if you do that. The subcontracts *must* have their own liability insurance and WCB (Worker's Compensation or WorkSafe in BC) coverage. It is intoxicating to think that if you hire only subcontractors, you get to avoid paying Pension and Employment Insurance remittances. This works well until the taxman comes snooping around during a random audit. The CRA and

IRS look very closely at janitorial companies because, sadly, so many people have abused the system.

The subcontractor/employee is off the hook in such a situation; it is always up to you to take responsibility. I have heard horror stories of companies that got fined seven years retroactively for remittances owed because the subcontractors couldn't prove they were not employees.

The subcontractor who laughs at CRA or IRS and doesn't pay taxes isn't doing themselves any favours either. Without proper tax documentation, they can't prove they have an income when they apply for a mortgage or buy a car. If they are seriously hurt, they cannot claim CPP (Canada Pension Plan or U.S. equivalent) or get a disability pension. Avoiding taxes is a shortsighted practice for both parties.

Of course there are legitimate reasons for using subcontractors. For one thing, they will have to shoulder all the staffing and manager complaints, which frees you up for marketing and other duties. They may also have specialized skills and equipment. Just weigh those advantages in the balance.

CHAPTER 6.

MARKETING

There are many different forms of advertising out there, even more options now with social media. I will simplify it and streamline the choices that work better for you and for the janitorial industry.

COLD CALLING

Everyone hates cold calling but even today, it still works.

In Chapter 2: Getting Started, you figured out what area of cleaning you want to focus on. Was it residential, commercial, light industrial? Scrubbing parking lots, washing windows, or cleaning carpets? You also made a list of potential customers. Keep this list fresh and updated, as it is your "cold call" list. You can add prospective clients to the list from the internet or Yellow Pages. Now, keep a pen and paper handy and start phoning.

Ask for the person in charge of building maintenance and/or the general manager, depending on the size of the store. Keep note of dates and whom you phoned and create a database of store managers and their extensions. Make sure you keep notes on the conversation so you can refer to them later, sometimes even years later.

Be simple and direct. I used to just say: "Hello Mr. _____. My name is Cora and my husband and I run a local cleaning company. I would like to make an appointment to meet you and give you a quotation."

Don't run on and on. Nine times out of ten they will say, "No, I am happy with my current cleaning company." End the conversation by asking permission to mail them a business card and letter. They will probably be polite and say yes, but then get off the phone. Always thank them for their time – you never know when you will meet them again and you will leave a favorable impression. Remember to actually follow up with the letter and card.

When you do make contact, don't say, "Hello your floors are really dirty, would you like a quotation?" That is insulting to the manager. Just ask them nicely if they would be interested in a quotation. They didn't get their jobs by being stupid in the first place; so leave it to them to give you an opening.

We hit the jackpot right away: one week after our move, we looked at the floors at a major department store near our home. They were filthy, so we asked to speak to the manager and he took us in right away. It turned out he had just fired his janitor the day before for coming into work drunk.

The next day I wrote out a quote and contract. I took a little nap on the couch before I left to deliver the contract, and let my six-year-old crawl around me a bit. When I arrived at the store, the manager hired us and we signed the contract without a hitch. When I got home, I looked in the mirror and saw my child had stuck baby barrettes randomly all over my hair. Either the manager didn't notice or he was too polite to say anything, but I was mortified!

When we presented ourselves as a husband and wife team who lived in the neighborhood and had children, the clients knew we were more than just a fly-by-night operation. They were tired of empty promises and were happy to give contracts to a stable family who had everything to lose but a lot to gain by making the customer happy. Don't underestimate the value of that.

While I am a firm believer in dressing for the occasion, don't wear a suit and tie to the interview. Who are you trying to kid? Be well groomed with a nice golf shirt and pressed casual pants and clean shoes, with similar attire for women. Have a presentable briefcase and presentation folder. Save the suit and tie for the ceremony where you are presented with your Chamber Entrepreneurial Award.

TRADE SHOWS

These are a lot of fun and tax deductible, and attending them gives you time for sight seeing that you will normally not be able to do. On the other hand, people in the cleaning industry tend to circulate and the person you made friends with at the ACME stand might be working for XYZ Company years later. Unless there is a breakthrough in technology or cleaning chemicals, all these trade shows start looking the same after a while.

The ISSA/Interclean Trade Show is the largest in the world. In previous years it has had Colin Powell and Margaret Thatcher as keynote speakers. I recommend attending those seminars and taking notes at each show. I remember clearly Colin Powell saying, "The United States has a God-given right to rule." Okay, we won't go there, it's not polite to discuss politics.

Why am I telling you this story? To give you an example of how your world will broaden once you are in business. You will get a chance to travel, meet some terrific people, and maybe have some adventures on the way. Just balance it with the upfront cost of travel.

We had the nicest times at trade shows with Bob and Burma Silbaugh, who ran Kleenco Cleaning Systems out of Kent, Washington. They were our main suppliers. My favorite trade show was in Atlanta, Georgia, where they took us to Stone Mountain. It has a sculpture carved right on the mountainside. I had my first martini in Atlanta!

Trade shows do become mutual admiration societies after a while, so only go every couple of years to keep the experience fresh. The flights, admission fees, hotels, meals etc. are very expensive and it takes valuable time away from your own company.

WEBSITE

Invest in a simple website. WordPress (see link in Resources chapter) and similar companies offer reasonable templates. You can also ask a design student to build one for you. My mantra is "Keep It Simple." Include your contact address, maybe a photo of your key team, information on the different types of jobs you can do, some testimonials, and contact information for quoting. Change it up for specials, or different cleaning tips to keep it fresh. I wouldn't put too many fixed prices on it, maybe just short-term specials.

Please check the spelling and grammar before you launch the site. I am a stickler for this and I often groan at some of the mistakes made by reputable companies. On publishing of this book, the person who runs Masterpiece

Floor Maintenance now has "Maintence" on their website.

SOCIAL MEDIA

In the past five years, social media has exploded around the world. Businesses need social media in order to appear professional, authentic, and modern. Even if you've never touched social media before, here are a few quick tips to get you started. Find all the links in the Resources chapter.

FACEBOOK

Your Facebook page will be the absolute core of your social media presence. It is completely free to make, and even if you don't plan on spending money to advertise on it, it is important to have a page set up so that people searching for you on Facebook can find you.

Fill in as much information as you can about your company and your business. Pretend you are decorating your storefront or your company webpage; inaccuracies and mistakes on your Facebook page will reflect poorly on your business as a whole. Go through your profile and fill in as much detail as you can.

On your page, you have the freedom to talk about anything you want. You can focus on news articles related to the cleaning industry, you could promote special deals, or upload photos of your new equipment or office. Remember, social media isn't just an advertising network. Avoid talking exclusively about your product or company and mix it up by having normal conversations with your followers.

At least initially, I would recommend you put some

money into Facebook advertising to get your number of followers up. The more people who follow you the more your posts will be seen. Run a "like" campaign for the first month and try to get your number of likes to at least 100. Invite all your friends and family to "like" your page.

TWITTER

Twitter is just as important, if not more so, than Facebook. Twitter will let you communicate almost constantly with your followers, and you can use it to direct people to your Facebook page or your website.

Use no more than two #hashtags per tweet. Hashtags can help your tweet get noticed, but having too many will make you look #very #obnoxious. Search your hashtag before you use it to get a general sense of how popular it is.

If you are tweeting about a blog post, news article, or anything someone else did, make sure to @mention their Twitter handle so they will see it. This is common courtesy in the Twitter world.

Post often, but not too often. Finding a posting frequency is important because you want to talk to your followers on a consistent basis, but not enough for them to "burn out" and get tired of you. I recommend 2-3 Facebook posts per week and 3-5 Twitter posts per day.

EMAIL MARKETING

Email marketing (email newsletters) is actually still one of the most effective ways to reach out to your customers. Social media may be the most popular thing, but email marketing has always brought in a lot of opens, click-throughs, and leads.

Creating an Email Newsletter Template

The easiest way to do this is to use one of the many free email-sending websites available. Constant Contact, Mailchimp, and Vertical Response are all solid choices and offer a free or trial version for you to test your email before you send it out. Each of these is fairly user-friendly and provides many different resources and templates to get started. You have free reign over the design of your email, but your email MUST have the following:

- The name, address, and contact information of your business.
- An "unsubscribe" button that lets people opt-out of your newsletters.

This will help make your email compliant with anti-spam legislation in both Canada and the United States.

Links to all of the above can be found in the Resources chapter.

Writing the Email Newsletter

You can use your newsletter for a variety of different things. You can write personal stories about your cleaning business or your company's origins to build a stronger relationship with your customers. You can have a weekly list of general cleaning tips to establish your business as a leader in the industry. You can even use it to promote your rates and offer discounts to your loyal followers. What you write about is up to you.

BUILDING YOUR LIST

Hopefully you'll have an email list of all of your current

and past customers so you have a base with which to start. If not, start collecting emails from your customers, your clients, your suppliers, and anyone else who might be interested!

However, if you're starting your business in Canada or sell to people in Canada, then the new anti-spam legislation in Canada will put a major damper on your efforts. As a business, you are not allowed to send anyone an email unless they have explicitly stated they want to receive your emails (generally through an online form).

If someone has done business with you, requested information from you about your company, or given you a business card, this counts as implied consent and is adequate until July 1, 2017. You can still send them emails until that time. But after that date, implied consent is no longer enough, and you will need explicit consent from each person you want to include on your list.

Although email marketing has definitely become more difficult and limited with the new laws, this doesn't mean you should avoid it. In fact, companies that do email marketing well in this new environment will have an advantage over all their competitors.

CHAPTER 7.

ACCOUNTING

I took some accounting and bookkeeping courses at the Invergarry Learning Centre, Kwantlen College and the Academy of Learning, all in Surrey, British Columbia. Each of those courses was unstructured, meaning I had the freedom to come and go within a certain timeframe. Every time I had a couple of hours free while my children were at school, I would run in and work on a course. You will want to get some training right away; don't wait until your first year of business is over, as that will be too late. You might be bankrupt by then, or perhaps will have made so much money that you have a huge tax bill to pay!

Yes, you can hire a bookkeeper, but there is nothing like being able to create your own accounting reports at any time. In the beginning you want to keep your pulse on your business. You should be able to read a balance sheet as well as a profit and loss statement and always know where you stand with your accounts receivable and accounts payable.

Invest in accounting software that includes payroll so you can create your own T4s or W-2 forms (income tax slips) to give your employee at the end of the year, as well as your own Records of Employment when an employee quits. I am familiar with both AccountEdge and Sage (Simply Accounting). These programs are not that expensive when you consider the time you save putting everything into spreadsheets or (gasp) a shoebox for the accountant at year-end. Remember these programs are just glorified spreadsheets; make them work for you, not the other way around. In other words, don't get intimidated or overwhelmed by them. You control the information that comes in and out of them.

When you take on a new contract, please remember that you will probably clean for one month before invoicing and then hope that your invoice will be paid within 15 days (though it will probably take 30). Always keep that in mind when planning your cash flow! That means if you start a contract January 1, you will have to come up with payroll for January 15, January 31, February 15 and probably February 28 – all before receiving payment for that contract. You will also be paying government remittances (Employment Insurance, Canada Pension and/or Income Tax) on behalf of those employers on February 15. Please see Resources chapter for links.

Always estimate those remittances ahead of time so you know exactly what to expect and include that amount if you are approaching your bank manager for an increase in credit limit.

LEASE VERSUS LOAN

At some point in time you will need to get a solid van and some buffing machines, scrubbing machines, vacuum cleaners or even carpet cleaning machines.

In my experience, leasing is not the best way to secure that equipment. When you sign a lease, you are stuck with the equipment if you lose a contract in the meantime. There is a usually a huge buy-out at the end of the term. Leasing used to offer a good tax advantage years ago but it's not worthwhile anymore. Yes, you can write off the lease payments as an expense, but you also can write off any depreciation if you decide to buy.

Unless you want to run a maid service or service small residential/commercial stores, you will need a van. The van will get smelly, and a lot of things roll around and spill. A car won't do except for quoting, buying smaller supplies, or banking/business meetings.

In my opinion you are much better off scraping together a down payment and buying a one- to three-year-old van (no older) and paying it off. Don't buy a brand new one, even if it has a fantastic warranty, because vehicles are so well built these days that nothing will break during the first year anyway. You lose too much in depreciation the instant you drive a new vehicle off the lot. If you do buy, you can always sell the van off later because you aren't trapped into a lease.

Equipment, on the other hand, will probably have to be replaced after the life of the lease. In the meantime, take very good care of your equipment. We've lost so many motors over the years because our supervisors didn't watch the oil and other fluids. It wasn't their property, after all.

PAYROLL

I have created a simple tool that factors in the primary payroll costs to give an approximate value on what your real cost per hour is. The laborers will get minimum wage but the lead hands and supervisors incrementally more. In 2014 the minimum wage in BC was $10.25 per hour.

You can always give your staff raises after the three-month trial period but you can't reduce the wage. It is a very cutthroat industry and you will never be able to pay the laborer much more, but try to incorporate pay raises when they get promoted. This spreadsheet does not include income tax, which is not an expense to you, but you must remit it monthly along with both the employee and employer's portion of CPP (Canada Pension Plan) and EI (Employment Insurance). It is only an approximate tool and does not include any medical or health premiums you may choose to pay. You can download the tool on my website, http://coraschupp.com.

If you only have one or two employees and can't afford accounting software in the beginning, the CRA (Canada Revenue Agency) has created a handy payroll deductions tool, a link for which is available in the Resources chapter. It uses the most updated tax tables, and not only figures out your employee's pay stub, but also tells you exactly how much the paycheck actually cost you. It may surprise you to see the difference between what the employee actually gets and how much you pay in total. Experiment with it using different salaries and you can see how the tax levels jump up. For you non-Canadian readers, I'm sure each of your respective governments has similar tools on their websites. Check out the IRS website for more information.

It might sound crazy, but put *yourself* on the payroll plan right away. That's right: begin paying taxes right away! Nothing kills a business faster than finding out at the end of the year that (heaven forbid) you made a profit, and now you have to double your installment payments.

BANKING

If you have taken out a loan, or arranged for an overdraft or line of credit, your bank manager will be looking at certain ratios on your records. For example, they will check whether your balance sheet owns about twice as much as what is owed. Any less could mean you have a potential problem with cash flow.

However, bank managers tend to dislike seeing a higher ratio. I was surprised at that too, but if a bank manager sees too much money in the bank verses accounts payable, he is going to see signs of stagnancy. Cash flow is called that because it is supposed to flow and not dam up, which is why cash is referred to as "liquid." Extra funds should be diverted to more equipment, more training, and newer vehicles. A business is like a plant in that it *has* to grow. Something that is not growing is ultimately dying.

Keep in mind that when you apply for a loan, your bank will probably want a list of receivables and will generally take 75% or less as the borrowing amount on your overdraft or loan.

A lot of people don't like using credit, but if you control it, it is a good tool to use. If you have a good credit rating and relationship with the bank manager, the day will come when you get a phone call and are offered a new large contract or chain of stores. You will need that sudden cash flow to prepare yourself; otherwise what are you going to do? Say, "No I can't take on this job, go somewhere else?" Someone else will be there to grab that opportunity.

OTHER ACCOUNTING TIPS

Find yourself a mentor. Your cleaning or equipment supplier will vie for the spot of "second best friend." (After your bank manager.) He or she wants to make money, and the only way to do that is to make sure you are making a profit. They will probably put on free seminars and will always be available to answer questions.

Download a template to create professional-looking invoices. Dollar store hand-written invoices don't cut it anymore. To download a sample invoice, please visit my website.

CHAPTER 8.

QUOTING

Quoting can make or break your business, so listen up. That applies to any business, especially the service industry. Keep notes on all your costs and listen for what the competition charges.

When you start negotiating with a prospective client, never ask them what they are currently paying. If they offer the information, that is great, but it is very unprofessional to ask upfront.

Once you have worked out a price, don't back down on it. If the prospective client says, "That is more than what I am paying now," please do not offer to match their current price because then it looks like you overcharged to begin with, which sets the wrong tone.

What you can do is negotiate duties. For example, say, "I can knock off $100 per month, but that means only emptying the garbage weekly or vacuuming every second day." That way you both keep your dignity intact. You should also be open to any suggestions. You want to get your foot in the door. After six months, a year, or when you are more familiar with your client, you can ask for a reasonable increase, but don't be upset if you don't get it.

This will give you more experience for the next time you quote.

Companies always want a monthly quote so they can do their own budgeting. You may wish to set up an hourly charge for unusual jobs (cleanups from break-and-enters, spills, floods, or before special meetings) and set it out clearly in the contract. Fees should be negotiated well ahead of time.

When writing the contract, or even sending the potential client a short email, please don't say "Hi" if you don't know them. It is spelled H-E-L-L-O. Also, take my advice and never use the term "guys." I will cringe and then I will follow you and find you.

Obviously, you can do whatever you want, but why spend the money buying my book if you don't want to take my advice?

If you start out with one small office and are doing the cleaning yourself, keep track of your hours for the first couple of months. For instance, how long does it take for one person to clean one bathroom? These are called man-hours. Tally them up over a couple of months and find the average. That will be the magic number that helps you quote on larger jobs. Take those hours, multiply by the average hourly wage and add another 20% or so for CPP, EI, WCB, statutory holidays and vacation pay.

At this point you should also have a good idea of the average amount of cleaning supplies you use per month. Make sure to build that into your quote, as well as your insurance, vehicle, and office expenses.

Your buffing machines will need propane and oil; your van will need gas, insurance and maintenance, as will your equipment. Floor squeegees are expensive and obvious, but little things like floor scrapers will add up if you aren't careful. Build in your own profit and add around 10% for error. Once you have a monthly amount you are comfortable charging, ask around for what the going rate is. Most responsible clients I know will ask for three quotes and take the one in the middle. They've learned not to just take the lowest one because often you get what you pay for.

Once you get a feel for the price you want to charge, you can divide the cost by the number of square feet to get an ideal price.

ECONOMIES OF SCALE

Bear in mind the larger the store, the better the economies of scale. Whether you clean a tiny convenience store or a large grocery store, you still have to drive to the site and unload the equipment. Costs like phone lines and insurance are known as "fixed" because they remain the same regardless of the job, but you will be able to negotiate a lower price for items such as soap and wax if you buy in bulk. Remember when you first bought a box of laundry detergent and noticed that a two-pound box was cheaper than double the price of a one-pound box? This is known as economies of scale and it is very important to understand when you start quoting for larger stores.

A store that is 2,000 square feet is not going to cost twice as much to clean as a store that is 1,000 square feet. Legally you have to pay an employee for four hours per shift, so it is more economical in the long run to get a larger store rather than two or three little ones because it takes so much time to travel, unload and setup, reload the van and travel to the next job site.

On my website, you can download a sample quote for your use. Make sure you date it, and give a valid length of time the quote is good for, such as 90 days.

CHAPTER 9.

MANAGING

This chapter deals with general management issues and is transferable to any type of business. Most of it is, when you think of it, general common sense.

POACHING

One thing I cannot stand is a poacher; I won't have anything to do with one. A poacher is someone who goes after your clients. While I have not had too much trouble with competitors trying to steal my staff, I recommend that you keep your information close to your vest, including contracts, pricing, leasing, and customer contacts.

When we were cleaning for a major department store, not only did we have to clean all 13 floors, we also had separate contracts for the bakery and meat departments. The meat department had especially pristine cleaning standards and was expensive because we needed high-pressure power washers. Each night the grinders and cutters had to be taken apart and steam cleaned. Thus we had 13 pressure washers under lease.

One day, one of our staff went to the store manager directly and complained that she hadn't had a raise in three years (which was not true). She said she could undercut our contracts and handle them herself. Even though I had proof of her raises (read my notes on keeping a paper trail), and the contracts weren't up for renewal, she was awarded the contracts.

Guess what? Shortly after she signed the lease on 13 new pressure washers, the store decided they would do their meat department cleaning in-house. She was stuck with all that equipment and was surprised that I wouldn't talk to her or invite her over anymore. Karma is a bitch, isn't she?

EQUIPMENT

The cost of insuring all of our scrubbing and buffing machines was far too expensive. Using that money, we would have been able to pay for a new piece every four years, and by that time, they needed replacing anyway. Instead, we decided to increase the insurance coverage for the work van. It covered whatever equipment was in the van at the time, and that worked out well.

One day before we left for a holiday, I mailed the final payment check on a propane-powered buffing machine. On the way to the airport, one of our supervisors called saying that while they were unloading the equipment to clean a 7-11 corner store, someone had stolen the buffer. The thief must have been watching and happened to have a large van of their own because the buffers were large, heavy, and bulky. In a few minutes our investment was gone. Watch your equipment diligently.

Take the time to train your staff carefully on how to properly use the equipment. Better yet, set up a training system, create a checklist of duties (e.g. change oil, clean battery posts), and make sure each new employee has been shown how to load and unload, properly use the equipment, and sign off on the checklist. Make sure your employees wear hearing protection, and ensure there are a variety of scrubbing pads and other basic supplies available so your workers never run out and you won't have to make a midnight trip.

Back when we were very new in the business, we were cleaning a grocery store along with one of our young new hires. We warned him that the loading ramp was very difficult to negotiate and had no barriers. Guess what? Two hours later our scrubbing machine was laying upside down in the parking lot, wheels spinning. The young man started crying so I took him home and made him breakfast. No one was hurt (except the machine, which was totaled), but you know what? People are more important than things and it would have served no purpose to make him feel worse than he already did.

I wasn't always so soft! We had another van equipped with hoses and heavy-duty carpet cleaners. We sent one young man out to do a carpet about 20 miles away. Ten hours later he returned with one invoice with payment, but the van was out of gas and all the cleaning solvent was gone. He obviously went into business for himself that day and pocketed all the cash but we couldn't prove it. We didn't use him again.

Always keep two checklists: one for regular equipment maintenance and one for staff duties. I didn't attach a checklist for equipment because there are too many different types. But I know for sure that they all need oil, and lots of it. These checklists can be updated daily, weekly, monthly, or yearly but always keep track of them. They can be used to prove staffing and will isolate problems or weaknesses in your organization. No one likes paperwork, especially when they are busy doing their jobs, so keep it as simple as possible. You can download a sample staff duties checklist from my website.

SCRUBBERS AND BUFFERS

Make sure you buy the right auto scrubber for the job; it will save you a tremendous amount on manpower. If it is too small, it will quickly wear out, plus it will require multiple passes up and down hallways. On the other hand, if it is too large you will have a lot of trouble navigating corners and aisles. A good scrubber should be able to cover 20,000 square feet per hour.

Choose a scrubber that is easy to run without a lot of bells and whistles. Try to find something sturdy that can be taken in and out of your van fairly easily. You will need a good solid mobile ramp to get your scrubber in and out in case there are no loading ramps at the location you are cleaning. Get yourself plenty of bungee cords to keep the equipment from moving around while you are driving.

We always used battery-operated ones that could run for at least four hours per charge. They were self-propelled and could go forward and reverse and had a multi-stage vacuum motor with large recovery and solution tanks. The batteries and mechanical parts should be easily accessible.

We used propane-powered buffing machines so we always made sure there were extra propane tanks on site and we had them in locked cages in the back of the store as they do smell a bit.

EQUIPMENT SUPPLY COMPANIES

I would like to recommend two very reputable companies that we used: Kleeno Cleaning Products for cleaning supplies and Coyote Equipment, for our scrubbing machines, both out of Washington, USA. The owner of Coyote Equipment developed a scrubbing machine that ran on propane and significantly boosted our business. His final creation was so ugly that he named it "Coyote." This name comes from an old army story about a man who went out on the town and went home with a woman he had picked up for the night. When he woke up, she was sleeping on his shoulder, and she was so frighteningly ugly in the light of day that he chewed his arm off rather than wake her up so that he could escape, coining the term "Coyote Ugly." There I go being politically incorrect again.

    Kleenco Products Inc.
      Bob Silbaugh
    6408 S 196th St
    Kent, Washington 98032-1169
    (253) 872-8787
    kleenco.com

    Coyote Cleaning Systems
      Jim and Mary O'Connor
    7208 210th S.W
    Edmonds, Washington 98026
    (800) 777-0454
    coyotescrubber.com

GOODWILL IS VALUABLE

A man's reputation and a woman's virginity have one thing in common; they can only be sold once. Be honest and scrupulous in all your dealings.

    Here are a few situations that we witnessed:

    One grocery store we had the pleasure of dealing with had a very nice and generous owner. His produce manager owned a horse, and sometimes when boxes of carrots would get soggy but not rotten he would request them for his horse.

This went on for quite a while but for some reason the owner got suspicious and put his hand into the box of carrots. Out came a pound of coffee!

The manager had to be sacked on the spot to send the message out that this behavior was not tolerated. He was making $45,000 a year, which was a lot of money in the late 1980s (honestly, it still is) and he threw it away on a pound of coffee. What is the moral of the story? Don't break your trust with your client.

Another time, we were asked by a department store client to fire one of our employees because he stole a roll of toilet paper worth about 25 cents. I don't know what he was thinking – he said he had a cold and grabbed it – nonetheless we had to let him go.

One of our mechanics was fixing a buffing machine in the back of a grocery store when he got hungry. He saw a banana perched nicely on top of the garbage bin and ate it. The client saw him and marched him out of the building. Very embarrassing for a decent family man who figured it was thrown out anyway, but there you go.

Loyalty is very important. If you have the cleaning contract for XYZ Groceries, don't let the manager see a shopping bag from Acme Groceries in your van. Let the manager see you or your family purchasing groceries from his store. It seems like a little thing, but sometimes actions speak louder than words.

Never put all your eggs into one basket. We learned this the hard way when we invested heavily in a grocery store chain in British Columbia. We had signed up for equipment leases of $8,000 per month (on our line of credit) when they suddenly pulled the contracts from us. We were completely devastated but we had to keep on going.

After the whole debacle, we quickly found out our stress was down, we had fewer staffing problems, and our profit margin remained the same. The grocery chain was a huge bubble and had very little substance left after it popped. We did survive, but after that point, we always diversified and made sure we had a variety of different contracts and businesses and never put ourselves in that situation again.

CHAPTER 10.

TROUBLE SHOOTING AND PROBLEM SOLVING

These are the biggest tips for success I want to impart to you before you stop reading and start taking action.

Use free resources (other than this book). Use the public library; they all have the internet now and you can find a lot of information on sourcing suppliers, etc.

Join your local Chamber of Commerce and go to a function at least once a month; the networking will be invaluable. It is a relaxed way to pass along business cards, meet new friends, and hopefully encourage everyone to give each other work. No one really wants to give business to out-of-towners when they can support their local business instead.

Don't spend a lot of money on fancy stationary or logos, but do keep your van, equipment and clothes clean. You are your own billboard for cleanliness, so to speak.

Don't spend a lot of money on lawyers except when you incorporate. Forms are actually much simpler than they appear, and by making annual filings and reports, you will save a lot of money.

The night before each shift, check over your calendar and shopping management needs. Gather all your necessary items and leave them by the front door (documents, contracts, broken items for replacement, etc.) and plan your route. You will surprise yourself with the amount of time, gas, and frustration you will save, and you will hit the ground running in the morning. A few minutes of planning will make all the difference in your success.

You will experience some "growing pains" and this is normal and to be expected. I had terrible shin pain at night as a child and ended up being 5' 11". There is going to be a transition period between being a small mom-and-pop business, and a full-scale operation, just like when your body changed from being a teenager to an adult. You are in fact cutting your teeth on a small business, but as I mentioned before, a business has to grow or die, just like human beings.

People used to ask me if there is such a thing as "being in the right place at the right time." I say no. It is up to you to make things happen.

CHAPTER 11.

KEEPING PERSONAL RELATIONSHIPS INTACT

I'm going to mention something that is never brought up in the seminars, and that is the importance of having a strong relationship with your partner or family at home.

As mentioned before, one of the challenges of running a janitorial services company is that you have to get your supplies, do your banking and paperwork, maintain your equipment, and interview new staff during the day, while the bulk of the actual janitorial work is done in the evenings and on weekends. You will have to oversee the majority of it in the beginning, and even when you've passed those responsibilities on to others, you need to always be available to oversee the work. That means phone calls throughout the night (so-and-so hasn't shown up, we ran out of propane, we ran out of soap, we have a flat tire and we're stuck on the highway, we lost the keys, the list is endless).

Being brought up in Canada with a European background, I never got used to waking up in the morning to a table full of workers who had been invited over for breakfast. Don't get me wrong! They were all great people and

I had no issues with them, but it took its toll on my health after being up all night with a baby. I do consider myself a hospitable person and there was always a pot of coffee on, but lines should have been drawn.

Once my husband had a salesman in the kitchen when our first-born threw up all over the floor. My husband told me, "Take the child somewhere else, we are doing business here." So I replied, "How about you go downstairs to do business, and I'll stay in the kitchen and take care of our child, otherwise you can help clean up." Needless to say, they made a beeline for the office. Shortly afterwards, we rented our first office off-premises.

You will have to carry the weight of the family on your shoulders, so please take good care of your loved ones. Don't berate them if something doesn't get done; play with the kids, spend time with them, do fun stuff on the weekends, or just hang around and relax. Make sure to get enough rest yourself. Never put so much on your plate that you lose your temper, get sick, or burn out. IT IS NOT WORTH IT!

The chickens always come home to roost, so if you take your frustrations out on your family, you will find yourself very lonely at the end of your life. All the money and success you've accumulated will only resemble a pile of ashes.

CHAPTER 12.

CHALLENGES

When we told our friends we were quitting our day jobs, selling our home, and taking our (then) two small children into the big unknown, they said we were crazy. We were warned of all the potential dangers of raising children in the big city. We were told there were thousands of people looking for work and that every second person wanted to start a business. We were told that four out of five businesses fail within five years.

I was told that I would never make anything of myself because my Dad was an alcoholic, which made me a "bad seed." On top of that, they looked down on me because I left home at 16 and had no college degree.

What they didn't tell me is that in Canada, a person is judged for what they *do*, not for where they come from. We don't have class systems that other countries use to drag their citizens down. Always keep your head up and be proud of who you are and where you came from. Mind you, in Terrace, where I graduated from high school, if you even hinted to someone that they were not good enough, they might drag you behind the KFC and beat you up.

I'm kidding. Sort of. The biggest sin you could commit back then was pretending to be someone you were not.

Before I quit my job to start the business, I jokingly told my boss that in six months I would end up on a park bench on skid row drinking out of a brown paper bag. He laughed and said, "Cora, you will never end up on a park bench, I know you and I know you will succeed." You only need a couple of positive voices to keep you heading in the right direction.

Once we started working in Surrey, we ran into a whole new set of problems. Employees were poaching our contracts, creating "Vicarious Liability issues" through dishonesty, and the competition was undercutting our quotes using illegal and immoral practices. "Vicarious Liability" means if you allow your employ to drive your company van, and he runs a red light while intoxicated, you could personally be held responsible for any damages that result. Worst of all, larger customers were turning a blind eye to these practices in order to obtain lower bids for themselves, thus reneging on their corporate responsibilities.

Once we obtained the larger grocery store contracts, the competition started waiting in the parking lot to pay our brand new employees to not show up for their first day of work!

Unscrupulous and illegal acts aside, we faced many other issues due to the nature of janitorial work. The biggest challenge in the janitorial industry is that when the client opens the office on Monday morning, they won't notice the sparkling windows or freshly washed floors, but they will always notice the one garbage can that was missed or the one dirty spot on the wall.

"Your cleaning crew didn't wipe that fingerprint on the wall by the copier on the 65th floor."

To top it all off, if anything went missing, no one ever blamed their own messy desk; they automatically accused the janitor. That is the nature of the beast, unfortunately.

No one ever wants to admit it, but there is a lot of bribery going on in this industry. I was asked point blank by a prospective client if I would "slip something under the table for him" if he gave me the contract. We turned him down, and about a year later we read in the paper that he had been caught and put in jail.

We once had to fire one of our top-level managers who was transferred to another province to oversee the opening of a new store. Why? When he arranged the landscaping at the store, he requested a few trees should "drop off the back of the truck" in the vicinity of his new home. A nice young man, very well paid, and his career straight down the toilet. Was it worth it?

There were a lot of rumors floating around various supply centers about store managers being bribed with time-shares in Hawaii, including escorts if they gave the contracts to the janitor companies doing the bribing. They don't call it a "dirty business" for nothing, but I'm not naïve enough to believe it only goes on in cleaning businesses. Don't fall for it.

You many think I am putting a damper on your dreams, but I wouldn't be doing you any favors by not alerting you to the possibility that these situations might happen. They may never come up, but at least you are now aware of them and you will be better prepared if they should arise. It is possible to keep yourself clean in this dirty business.

CHAPTER 13.

MY OWN STORY OF STRUGGLES AND SUCCESS

As a woman and a mother, I encountered different challenges from men in similar positions. The practical reality was this: many times I would make the cold call, schedule the initial interview, prepare the proposal, and when it was time to meet the prospective client, he would go right over my shoulder and shake my husband's hand.

There were many occasions when I had difficulty with a vendor and would try to talk reasonably and calmly and get nowhere with them. All it took was my husband to phone back, shout a bit, and the situation would be instantly resolved. Sometimes there was no shouting from our end – just yes sir, no sir at the other end. That really bothered me but that was just how things were at the time, and probably still are.

I remember asking my teacher in the business management course I was taking about how he managed to balance his work and family. He looked puzzled at my question and asked, "What balance?" Obviously he had Betty Crocker waiting for him at home all dressed in an apron with a martini for him. I did not get any hot meals waiting for me!

Multitasking became an increasingly important skill as I became adept at negotiating prime interest rates with my banker over the phone in one hand, stirring the soup with the other, balancing baby on one hip, and shoving the dog out of the way with my foot!

I had a hard and fast rule that I tried to keep at home: no answering phone calls during dinner. I figured that it was only 20 minutes a day that all of us got to be together without any distractions. I told the kids that no one was allowed to answer the phone unless it was the Pope calling.

One dinner the phone rang, and my 4-year-old picked it up. "Are you the Pope?" she asked. It was a good thing it was one of our employers and not a client! We still share a laugh over that one.

As this chapter is named "My Own Story of Struggles and Success," I will share another very strange incident with you. We had a Ford Expedition under lease that we were proud of. The last row of seats was raised so only children could sit on it, and it got 11 miles to the gallon. I am the worst parker ever and I always got glared at in the parking lot.

One early morning, John, our sales manager, phoned us while we were still at home to tell us that the Ford had been stolen. Here's what happened:

Someone came to the front of the shop to fill out a job application form. Just then someone else started banging on the back shipping/receiving door. John left to open the back door, but no one was there. When he went back to the front, our car was slowly being driven out of the parking lot. It was a team of con artists and unfortunately the keys had been left out on the counter.

We decided to write the whole thing off and put a claim in to our insurance agency. A week later we figured it had been taken apart into a thousand pieces and resold.

One afternoon I was washing shelves and needed to go to the bank. Something told me to finish the shelving, so I took my time with that before leaving. I went to the bank and lo and behold, my Expedition was parked crookedly in the handicapped parking spot at the bank. The windows were down and someone's jacket and cell phone were on the seat.

I ran into the bank and called the security guard, who called the police. A plain-clothes officer came up to us and said, "This isn't your car, and there is a different license plate on it."

I replied: "Obviously they replaced the plates, but I recognize a certain scrape on the back. Open the glove compartment, you'll find some Arabic CDs and information from our summer camping site." Sure enough, they were there. The culprit was still standing in line at the bank and was apprehended. Now what were the chances of me being there right at the same time in that large city? If I had left a few minutes earlier (like I originally planned), I would have missed it entirely.

There is a lesson to this long and rambling story: keep your eyes open and be alert all the time. Keep focused on your business and keep your eyes on the prize.

In this book I have addressed the issues and challenges that both men and women entrepreneurs will have to face. These lessons are very important because it affects your family and their future.

Fast forward to 2014. Even now, I am sure you hear the same excuses and naysayers keeping you down. Here I am living proof that you can spit them all in the eye (please don't actually do this) and say that *you* have what it takes.

AWARDS

One of our suppliers decided to nominate us for the New Canadian Entrepreneur Awards in 1998 and we became one of the recipients under the service category.

My husband joked that he was the "New Canadian" and that I was the "Old Canadian." It was held in a fancy hotel in Vancouver and it was a very proud moment for both of us when we got the award.

I suspected (and still do), that while these awards look very nice hanging on the office wall, the people organizing these events make a lot of money off our backs. Not only did it involve new clothes, a new hairdo, formal photographs, and many other expenses, but we also had to buy our own tickets and an extra table for our friends and family.

The awards were a once in a lifetime and we had a lot of fun, but don't buy into this game if you don't have the money. Don't rationalize that these events, like trade shows, are tax deductible, because although they are, you don't pay taxes on money you haven't earned yet.

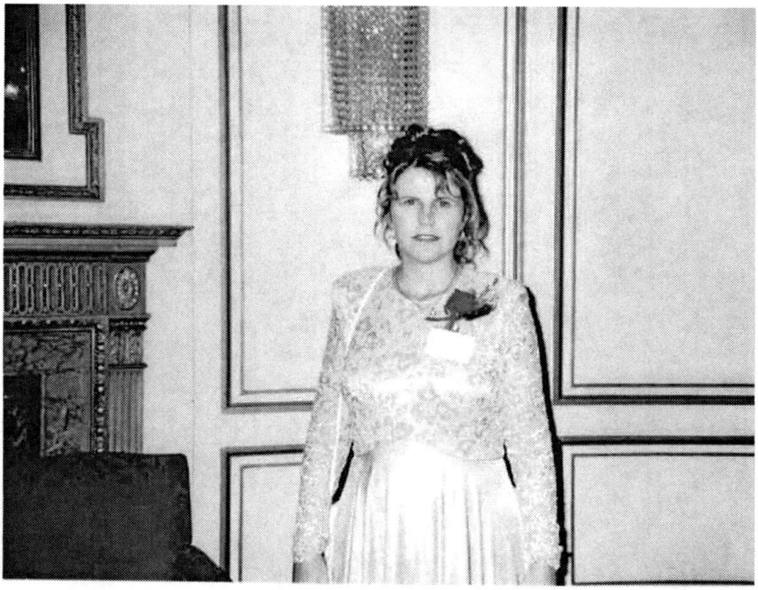

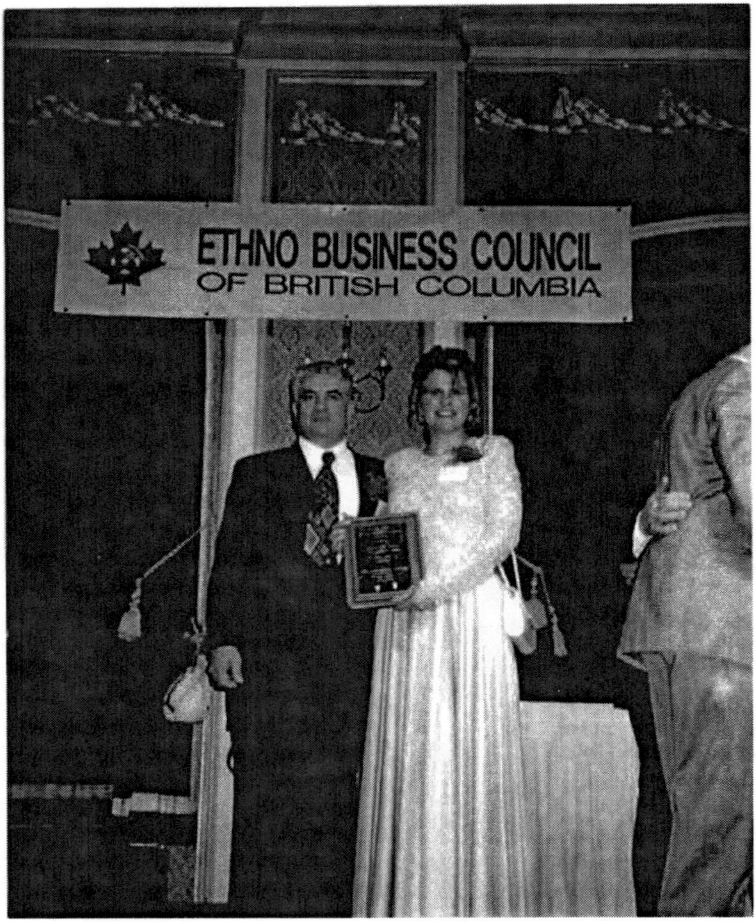
ETHNO BUSINESS COUNCIL
OF BRITISH COLUMBIA

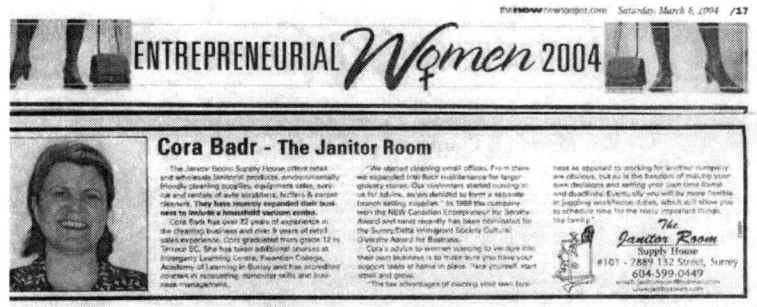

We were also nominated for the Surrey Cultural Diversity Award in 2004.

9TH ANNUAL CULTURAL DIVERSITY AWARDS FOR BUSINESS 2004

THURSDAY
MARCH 25
6:00 PM
TO
9:30 PM

SHERATON
GUILDFORD
HOTEL

PRESENTED BY
SURREY DELTA IMMIGRANT SERVICES SOCIETY

15269 104TH AVENUE
SURREY, B.C. CANADA

For us, the successes were more than just monetary or pride. We were just happy to be able to have a positive effect on the lives of those around us. Success can come in many different forms.

For example, one of our supervisors was with us for at least 15 years. He started with us at 18 with a row of earrings running up his ears and very long hair. Over the years he took on more and more responsibility and eventually became our right hand. He went to school during the day, worked for us in the evenings, and eventually became a lawyer. He is now a partner in a successful law firm in Nanaimo.

Seeing your staff do well is a type of success, too, isn't it? Nothing made me happier than seeing an employee drive into work in a new car or hearing that they were able to put a down payment on their own home.

CHAPTER 14.

ACTION PLAN

The actions I want you to take after reading this book are:

1. Make an appointment with your business loans bank manager. They will become your new best friend. I did say in the beginning that you do not need a lot of start-up capital, but before you grow too quickly you should meet your local bank manager to start a relationship with them. You don't want to wait until the last minute. They will offer you free seminars so you can get a feel for how the banking and credit systems work.
2. Find yourself a good accountant who will work *with* you, not *for* you; someone who understands that you are running a business and thus have little time or patience for unimportant interruptions. Visit with them every six months to track your profit and loss. Earlier in the book I said that you should be familiar with the bookkeeping process, but eventually you will be too busy to do it all. Pay someone to do your books, and pay yourself to run your business. Also,

your accountant will do your payroll and year-end taxes, which is another category altogether.
3. Find an answering service. We used one, and they always answered the phone professionally (without the noise of a screaming baby or a barking dog in the background) and well into the evening and weekends. That way, we could go to weddings or piano recitals without being disturbed. We would check for messages when we had a chance. The cost was reasonable and definitely worth it. I know more and more people use their smartphones for texting, but I am old school. There is nothing tackier than having your phone on the restaurant dinner table or during formal ceremonies. The world does not revolve around you and will manage just fine without you for half an hour or so. Show some class and your clients will respect you for it. An answering service still gives your client a human voice to address his/her queries, at least during the day. It doesn't hurt to price it out.

On the subject of phones, if your client or employee comes into your office to discuss something with you, give them the dignity of your time and attention. Look at them as if you are really listening. If the phone rings, ignore it. The person in front of you trumps the person on the phone. The phone will wait, just like dirty dishes.

4. Separate cleaning clothes for bathrooms, kitchen, and general office duties and keep them color-coded. Cross-contamination is a big issue, so make sure your staff is trained properly and not using the same rag they used on the toilet to wipe down the

telephone. Apparently 30% of the population gets sick from something they picked up at work.

5. Make sure your staff knows to empty the paper recycling boxes under each desk into the recycling bin and not the garbage. Yes, I have seen this happen. Why do you think the office staff takes the time to separate it? Sometimes what is obvious to you or me may not be obvious to your team.
6. Invest in a course on industrial cleaning at your local college. Nowadays, a janitor has to be part chemist, part engineer and part mechanic.
7. Find a cleaning supply company close by with a staff that you feel comfortable with. Saving a couple of dollars on a pail of soap is not worth the gas and time to drive another 20 miles out of the way, especially when it is 4:30 pm and you realize you have run out of stripper. You will need buckets, mops, several sizes of brooms, rags, window cleaner, and all-purpose cleaner. This will also include sanitizer.
8. You will also need a good quality vacuum cleaner. Do not be frugal on this. It is much cheaper in the long run to buy something for $500 that will last five years, than to buy something for $200 and have to replace it every year.
9. Also invest in both a Workplace Hazardous Materials Information System (WHMIS) course and a Shipping Hazardous Goods course. You will be handling a lot of chemicals, so keep yourself and your staff healthy. In the WHMIS course you will learn about MSDS (Material Safety Data Sheets).

A lot of people moaned and groaned when this system was enforced. Now I cannot imagine sending my work force out handling chemicals with no idea of what is in them, or how they react to the skin, eyes, and lungs. A binder of all chemicals must be on site, close to the eye station.

Each year you must provide each client with a Safety Standards reminder. You can download a sample of this letter on my website. It will also give you details about WHMIS or MSDS. Each chemical you carry will have an associated sheet that explains what is in it, and what to do if splashed in your eyes or accidentally swallowed. An example of a MSDS is available on my website

10. Take advantage of free courses. I took a lot of free courses from what used to be called the Federal Business Development Bank. It is now the Business Development Bank of Canada and I can't emphasize enough how much valuable information I got from them. They even offered mentoring where they would match me up with a volunteer with business experience. I don't remember his name but I do remember his advice: "Keep your information close to your vest." I didn't really get the impact of that statement at the time but sure do now. See the Resources chapter for a link to the Business Development Bank of Canada.

TEMPLATES

Throughout this book, I've mentioned various free templates that I created to help you launch your cleaning business. You can customize them with your own business name and logo. They include:

- Business budget
- Cleaning checklist
- Job application form
- Payroll planning tool
- Quotation
- Safety standards

You can download them from my website: http://coraschupp.com.
Enter the password: dirtybusiness
Good luck!

RESOURCES

CANADA

Business Registry Services (in B.C.):
www.bcregistryservices.gov.bc.ca

Business Registry Services (in Alberta):
http://www.servicealberta.gov.ab.ca/Consumers_Licenses.cfm

Business Registry Services (in Saskatchewan):
https://business.isc.ca/Pages/default.aspx

Business Registry Services (in Manitoba):
http://www.gov.mb.ca/business/registration/

Business Registry Services (in Ontario):
http://www.bdccanada.com/BDC/Corporate/Business_Registration_ON.htm

Business Registry Services (in Quebec):
http://www.registreentreprises.gouv.qc.ca/en/demarrer/immatriculer/default.aspx

Business Registry Services (in Nova Scotia):

http://www.novascotia.ca/sns/access/business/ready-register-business.asp

Business Registry Services (in New Brunswick):
https://www.pxw2.snb.ca/brs/docroot/start/landingPage.jsp

Business Registry Services (in Prince Edward Island):
http://www.gov.pe.ca/corporations/index.php

Business Registry Services (in Newfoundland and Labrador):
http://www.servicenl.gov.nl.ca/registries/companies.html

Business Registry Services (in Yukon):
http://www.community.gov.yk.ca/corp/inc.html

Business Registry Services (in Northwest Territory):
http://www.justice.gov.nt.ca/CorporateRegistry/CR_Partnership_BNReg.shtml

Business Registry Services (in Nunavut):
http://nunavutlegalregistries.ca/cr_index_en.shtml

Canada Revenue Agency payroll deductions online calculator:
https://apps.cra-arc.gc.ca/ebci/rhpd/startLanguage.do?lang=English

Government of Canada job bank:
www.jobbank.gc.ca

Canada Revenue Agency GST account registration:

www.cra-arc.gc.ca/tx/bsnss/tpcs/gst-tps/rgstrng/menu-eng.html

Business Development Centre in BC – GST account registration:
http://www.gst-tax.com/GST/HST_tax_British_Columbia.htm?gclid=CNeh-MGabsCFRCBfgodHTEAcw

Business Development Bank of Canada:
http://www.bdc.ca/en/Pages/home.aspx

Variance Permit (BC):
http://www.labour.gov.bc.ca/esb/facshts/averaging.htm

WorkSafe BC:
www.worksafebc.com

Workers' Compensation Board of Alberta:
http://www.wcb.ab.ca/

Saskatchewan Workers' Compensation Board:
http://www.wcbsask.com/

Ontario Workplace Safety and Insurance Board:
www.wsib.on.ca/

Workers' Compensation Board Quebec (Commission de la santé et de la sécurité du travail du Québec):
http://www.csst.qc.ca/en/Pages/all_english_content.aspx

Workers Compensation Board of Nova Scotia:
http://www.wcb.ns.ca/

WorkSafe New Brunswick: http://www.worksafenb.ca/

Workers' Compensation Board of Prince Edward Island: http://www.wcb.pe.ca/

Workplace Health, Safety & Compensation Commission of Newfoundland and Labrador: http://www.whscc.nf.ca/

Yukon Workers' Compensation, Health and Safety Board: http://www.whscc.nf.ca/

Workers' Compensation Board of the Northwest Territories and Nunavut: http://www.wscc.nt.ca/Pages/default.aspx

UNITED STATES

Department of Labor vacation pay requirements: www.dol.gov/dol/topic/workhours/vacation_leave.htm

Department of Labor variance permit/flexible schedules information: http://www.dol.gov/dol/topic/workhours/flexibleschedules.htm

Federal Tax ID application: www.apply-gov.us/tax-id

US employee deductions calculator: http://www.irs.gov/Businesses/Small-Businesses-&-Self-Employed/Understanding-Employment-Taxes

Internal Revenue Service:

http://www.irs.gov/Businesses/Small-Businesses-&-Self-Employed/Starting-a-Business

U.S. Job Bank:
www.ajb.dni.us

Pension plans:
www.usa.gov/Topics/Seniors/Retirement.shtml

Workers Compensation:
www.workerscompensation.com/

ONLINE AND SOCIAL MEDIA

Create a simple website:
www.wordpress.com

Create a Facebook page:
www.facebook.com

Create a Twitter account:
www.twitter.com

Email newsletter marketing:
www.constantcontact.com

www.mailchimp.com

www.verticalresponse.com

OTHER

Create a business plan:
www.plangenie.com

CONCLUSION

All the information in this book is gleaned from 20 years of practical experience. I sold my partnership in the business in 2005 and although I am no longer a part of Masterpiece Floor Maintenance Ltd., we did become very successful in a short period of time. As the old saying goes, "You can't argue with success," and times and people have not changed so much that this information is not just as fresh and valid as it was when we were young and green.

I wish you all the best in your own journey. Please feel free to email me with any questions you may have. I would love to hear from you and follow your own successes.

My email address is cora@coraschupp.com.

My website is http://coraschupp.com.

I never thought I would hear myself say this, but I hope you succeed in your own "dirty" business.